T0132225

Sean Vincent Goes Home

A LIFE STORY

The Luna Family

WestBow Press books may be ordered through booksellers or by contacting:

WestBow Press
A Division of Thomas Nelson & Zondervan
1663 Liberty Drive
Bloomington, IN 47403
www.westbowpress.com
1 (866) 928-1240

ISBN: 978-1-9736-4990-8 (sc)
ISBN: 978-1-9736-4991-5 (e)

Library of Congress Control Number: 2018915113

Print information available on the last page.

WestBow Press rev. date: 01/02/2019

Dedicated to Sean Vincent, *our tiny little hero,* and to all who supported our family and this little book that we pray will bring great hope to those in need.

It is Christmas Eve and my Mommy and Daddy have a special gift for my little sisters, Olivia, Maggie and me.

"We are going to have a little baby," said Daddy!

"Yay," I shouted! "I love babies! That is just what I want for Christmas!"

Olivia smiled and said, "I am happy because I want a baby for Maggie to play with."

Maggie just giggled. She didn't know a baby was on the way.

My Mommy and Daddy wanted to make sure our baby was healthy, so they went to the doctor.

The doctor used an ultrasound machine to take a picture of the baby in mommy's belly. He was able to tell that the baby was a boy.

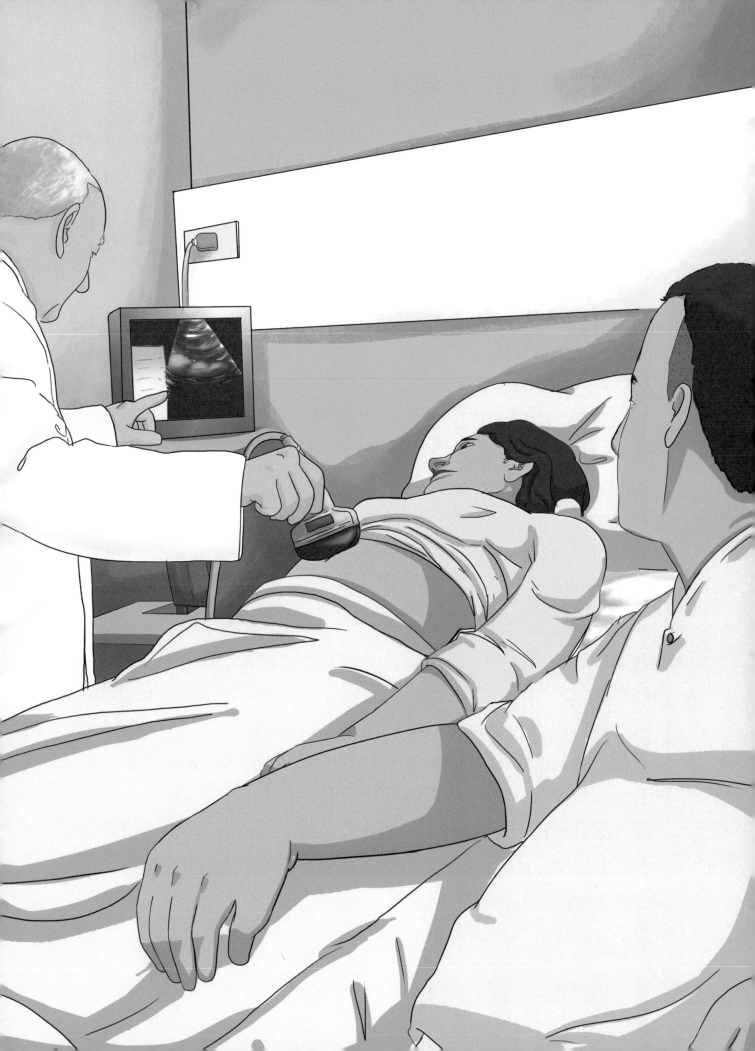

Daddy told Olivia, Maggie and me that we were going to have a baby brother and his name would be Sean.

"Yay! We are going to get to meet baby Sean soon!" Olivia shouted.

As Sean grew in my mommy's belly, she and daddy went to the doctor a few more times to make sure Sean was healthy.

During one visit, the doctor saw something that made mommy and daddy sad.

Baby Sean was sick.

My mommy and daddy were scared, but they trusted that God and their doctors would take good care of Sean.

Daddy told us "God loves children, but he does not love sickness in children. Sometimes He gives gifts to people like doctors, nurses and scientists to cure sickness. Sometimes, however, God needs to take them to heaven to cure the sickness himself."

And then he told us that Sean was very sick.

I cried a little and curled up tight as Daddy gave me a long hug.

"It's going to be okay, Luke," said Daddy. "We are going to get through this with God's help." Each night we prayed over Sean in mommy's belly and said:

"God please help Sean to be better in this world or in heaven, and if you have to take him to heaven, we would love to meet him first, but we understand if that can't happen."

Then we kissed mommy's belly and made the sign of the cross saying "we love you Sean and may Jesus bless you in the name of the Father and of the Son and of the Holy Spirit, Amen."

The day soon came for baby Sean to be born.

Daddy told us that when he was born, the nurses wrapped him in a baby blanket and placed him in daddy's arms.

Daddy held him close and kissed him.

Then mommy kissed Sean's little nose. She said it was soft and pink like velvet, just like Olivia and Maggie's noses when they were born (and mine too)!

Sean was beautiful.

My mommy and daddy's pastor was with them and he baptized Sean sprinkling him with holy water.

Soon, Olivia, Maggie and I got to meet Sean. He was very tiny and he lay very still.

We hugged Sean, kissed him, and asked God to make him better.

I held Sean tight as I said to Daddy "I know God needs to take Sean to heaven soon, but he is such a cutie, I could hold him forever."

Daddy smiled.

After a while, it was time to let God take Sean to heaven.

Mommy, Daddy, Olivia, Maggie and I each gave Sean one more kiss, and then his eyes closed. He looked so peaceful – just like he was sleeping.

"Are we going to take Sean home now, Daddy" I asked. "All children are supposed to come home," added Olivia.

"Sean is home," said Daddy. "He is home in the loving arms of God in heaven, and one day, God willing, we will all go home to heaven and be with Sean again."

Printed in the United States
By Bookmasters